Festivals of the World

AUSTRALIA

Gareth Stevens Publishing
MILWAUKEE

Written by
DIANA GRIFFITHS

Edited by
AUDREY LIM

Designed by
HASNAH MOHD ESA

Picture research by
SUSAN JANE MANUEL

First published in North America in 1999 by
Gareth Stevens Publishing
1555 North RiverCenter Drive, Suite 201
Milwaukee, Wisconsin 53212 USA

For a free color catalog describing Gareth
Stevens' list of high-quality books and multimedia
programs, call
1-800-542-2595 (USA)
or 1-800-461-9120 (Canada).
Gareth Stevens Publishing's Fax: (414) 225-0377.
See our catalog, too, on the World Wide Web:
http://gsinc.com

© TIMES EDITIONS PTE LTD 1999
Originated and designed by
Times Books International
an imprint of Times Editions Pte Ltd
Times Centre, 1 New Industrial Road
Singapore 536196
Printed in Singapore

Library of Congress Cataloging-in-Publication Data:
Griffiths, Diana.
Australia / by Diana Griffiths.
p. cm.—(Festivals of the world)
Includes bibliographical references and index.
Summary: Describes how the culture of Australia
is reflected in its many festivals, including
Melbourne Cup Day, Australia Day,
and Mabo Day.
ISBN 0-8368-2021-5 (lib. bdg.)
1. Festivals—Australia—Juvenile literature.
2. Australia—Social life and customs—Juvenile
literature. [1. Festivals—Australia. 2. Holidays—
Australia. 3. Australia—Social life and customs.]
I. Title. II. Series.
GT4890.G75   1999
394.26994—dc21   98-39036

1 2 3 4 5 6 7 8 9 03 02 01 00 99

CONTENTS

It's Festival Time . . .

Australians love festivals and holidays because they are times to be with their families and to have fun. From watching arts performances during the Adelaide Arts Festival to opening presents on Christmas in summer, Australians show the rest of the world their brand of fun—"Oz" style! Come **witness** dawn services carried out on Anzac Day and appreciate Aboriginal culture. It's festival time in Australia . . .

WHERE'S AUSTRALIA?

A ustralia is an island continent in the Southern Hemisphere and includes Tasmania, a smaller island that lies south of the mainland. Due to its location, Australia is often known as "the land down under," particularly by people in the Northern Hemisphere.

Who are the Australians?

A mother teaches her children that even small koalas must be handled cautiously.

The original inhabitants of Australia were the **Aborigines**. Since the arrival of Europeans in the eighteenth century, however, Aboriginal culture has suffered. Efforts are presently being made to protect Aboriginal culture and make up for the poor treatment Aborigines received after European **settlement**.

Today, Australia is a nation of immigrants. When it was a British colony, settlers from England, Scotland, Ireland, Italy, Greece, and Germany came to Australia. Chinese settlers have been coming to Australia since the discovery of gold there during the middle of the nineteenth century. Recently, however, more Asian families have arrived in the country.

AUSTRALIA

N

Melville Island
Bathurst Island •Darwin

INDIAN OCEAN

Gulf of Carpentaria

CORAL SEA

NORTHERN TERRITORY

•Cairns

Great Sandy Desert

Great Barrier Reef

QUEENSLAND

Tropic of Capricorn

WESTERN AUSTRALIA

Alice Springs•
Ayers Rock

SOUTH AUSTRALIA

Coober Pedy•

Brisbane•

Kalgoorlie•

NEW SOUTH WALES

Perth•

Great Australian Bight

Adelaide•

Sydney•
Botany Bay
■CANBERRA

Spencer Gulf

Kangaroo Island

VICTORIA

•Melbourne

Bass Strait

PACIFIC OCEAN

TASMANIA

•Hobart

Central Australia is a desert landscape but has some amazing natural features, such as Ayers Rock.

WHEN'S THE CELEBRATION?

*Turn the pages to
see more lovely
festival costumes.*

SUMMER

- ✪ **CHRISTMAS**
- ✪ **BOXING DAY**—A holiday popular in Australia for its sports events. The Sydney to Hobart yacht race starts on this day.
- ✪ **NEW YEAR'S DAY**
  - ✪ **AUSTRALIA DAY**—Also called Foundation Day, this holiday celebrates the arrival of the First Fleet in 1788.
  - ✪ **ADELAIDE ARTS FESTIVAL**—Held every two years in South Australia, it is the biggest arts festival in the Southern Hemisphere.

AUTUMN

- ✪ **GOOD FRIDAY**
- ✪ **EASTER**
- ✪ **ANZAC DAY**—Street marches and dawn services honor those who fought and died in wars.
  - ✪ **MAY DAY**—Celebrated in certain states as a holiday for workers.

Don't we look lovely in our pretty outfits?

Discover more about Aboriginal culture on pages 26 and 27.

WINTER

- ✪ **MABO DAY**—Celebrates a decision by the Australian High Court supporting Aboriginal land rights claims.
- ✪ **QUEEN'S BIRTHDAY**—Originally declared a holiday for convicts and settlers from the first years of settlement, a day is still set aside as a holiday in honor of the British monarch's birthday. Western Australia celebrates this occasion in October, whereas all other states celebrate on the second Monday of June.

SPRING

- ✪ **FLORIADE**—A citywide flower festival in Canberra.
- ✪ **MELBOURNE CUP DAY**— A famous horse race celebrated all over Australia on the first Tuesday of November.

CHRISTMAS

Christmas is a time for everyone to celebrate in Australia. For Australians who are Christians, religious services commemorating the birth of Christ bring out the true meaning of this joyful season. For others, Christmas is a time to be with family members, exchange gifts, and enjoy holiday festivities. An Australian Christmas is different from a traditional Northern Hemisphere Christmas because, in Australia, December is in the middle of summer.

Have you ever seen a Christmas stocking this large?

Gifts and parades

The best part of Christmas, especially for children, is exchanging gifts with family and friends. Weeks before Christmas Day, large stores have their own Santa Clauses to **amuse** children while parents shop for presents. There are Christmas parades, too, in which children especially enjoy taking part.

Left: All set for the parade.

Opposite: A Christmas parade in full swing.

8

People enjoying a Christmas meal.

Christmas feasts

People spend Christmas day enjoying their presents, visiting their neighbors and relatives, and preparing the Christmas meal, which is usually eaten in the afternoon. Around lunchtime, family members and friends gather to eat a delicious barbecue or seafood meal. Sometimes a traditional European Christmas feast is prepared, with roasted meats or turkey, baked vegetables, pies, and pudding.

Sports events

The day after Christmas is Boxing Day. Each year, Boxing Day heralds the start of major sports events. One such event is the Boxing Day test match, which is a cricket game played between Australia and another country. Huge crowds come out to relax, enjoy the sunshine, and watch cricket. Another big event is the Sydney to Hobart Yacht Race. Yachts leave Sydney Harbor bound for Hobart city, the capital of Tasmania.

Santa Claus up in the sky.

A Christian celebration

Although recent immigrants to Australia have brought with them new religions, Christmas is still regarded as a Christian event. Even people who do not go to church regularly attend special Christmas services alongside those who worship weekly. Australians who are not of any particular faith still celebrate Christmas according to Christian ideals of peace and **goodwill** toward all people.

Children dressed in nativity costumes.

AUSTRALIA DAY

In mid-January 1788, a fleet of British ships, known as the First Fleet, landed at Botany Bay. On January 26th, the fleet's captain, Arthur Phillip, established the first European settlement in Australia in the name of the British Crown. This settlement later became the city of Sydney. Australia Day celebrates the First Fleet's landing and the nation's establishment. Recently, Australia's Aboriginal population has protested on Australia Day against the occupation of their land by Europeans. Aborigines had lived in Australia long before Europeans arrived.

People dressed in festival outfits watching a reenactment of the First Fleet landing.

Australia Day activities

Above: Reenactment of the First Fleet landing.

Because Australia Day is in summer, many Australians celebrate by going to the beach or camping. Children make **damper** [DAM-puh], a type of bread made with flour, water, and *billy* [BILL-ee] tea. Billy tea is made in an open tin kettle over a campfire.

In the days leading up to Australia Day, many children visit historic sites or museums or create their own displays to show what Australia Day means to them. Flags are seen everywhere, and entertainers sing in schools and public places where people gather to enjoy the holiday.

Right: Ships celebrating Australia Day.

13

Captain James Cook at Botany Bay. Cook was an explorer and navigator, who had sailed the world's oceans.

Celebrating history

In 1770, Australia was first claimed in the name of the British Empire by Captain James Cook. In 1788, a settlement was formed near what is now Sydney. The British used this settlement as a prison colony. They also wanted its farmland to produce wheat and wool for the European market.

Governor Arthur Phillip was given the job of ruling the new colony. Life for convicts who had been transported to Australia was very hard. They constructed some of Australia's first buildings, which can still be seen in Sydney's historic area called The Rocks.

Governor Arthur Phillip.

Aborigines and Australia Day

Aborigines have been living in Australia for thousands of years, long before the arrival of the First Fleet. Since the establishment of white settlements, Aborigines have lost their traditional land, and their lifestyle and culture have also been affected.

Recently, Aborigines won the right to reclaim some areas of Australia as their own, but **disputes** over this right still occur, particularly between Aborigines and industries, such as mining and agriculture. Because of these disputes, some Aboriginal groups have chosen to mark Australia Day by protesting against the poor treatment of their people since the arrival of European settlers in 1788.

Think about this
Recently, Australia Day has become a time when people discuss the idea of Australia becoming a republic. Although Australia is an independent nation, it still has some ties to Britain, which more and more people think should be completely removed. Removing such ties would mean changing the flag, and agreeing on a new design is not easy.

The Aborigine in the center is blowing a *didgeridoo* [dij-uh-ree-DOO], which is a horn made out of tree branches.

THE ADELAIDE ARTS FESTIVAL

Since 1960, Adelaide has been home to the Adelaide Arts Festival. Artists from all over the world are invited to perform at this festival, which is held every two years. Dance, drama, classical and modern music, comedy, and opera are featured during this two-week celebration. This festival usually starts in late February and runs through to mid-March, so visitors to the city are able to enjoy the late summer weather while they watch the shows.

The Festival Center at Adelaide (*above*) and performers at the Adelaide Fringe Festival (*below*).

Adelaide — arts capital of Australia

Young people having a fantastic time at the Adelaide Arts Festival.

Although it is not the biggest city in Australia, Adelaide is certainly one of the most attractive. It can also lay claim to being the arts capital of Australia. Designed by Colonel William Light, the city is known for its wide streets, sandstone and bluestone buildings, and many parks and gardens. It is often called "the city of churches" because of the grand cathedrals and temples that make up the cityscape. A number of churches have been converted into theaters, and some of the events during the festival are held in these old buildings. Other events are held outdoors, taking advantage of the warm weather and large parklands surrounding the city. During the festival, those involved in the arts get together to discuss their ideas and meet people who might be interested in having them perform in other countries and at other arts festivals. Her Majesty Queen Elizabeth The Queen Mother is the current patron of the Adelaide Arts Festival.

Above: A performance in progress at the Fringe Festival.

Think about this

To introduce young people to the arts in Adelaide, performers use unusual and alternative venues to play music, dance, and show off their skills. Everyone is encouraged to join in. As part of the Fringe Festival, actors perform at schools in and around Adelaide or arrange for students to attend their performances.

The Adelaide Fringe Festival

While the Adelaide Arts Festival is going on, another festival is also held. This second festival offers an **alternative** to the larger, more expensive Arts Festival. It is called the Adelaide Fringe Festival, and it attracts hundreds of acts from all over the world who perform in small venues, sometimes in places as unlikely as a public parking lot. Anyone can perform at the Fringe Festival, and the shows offered vary tremendously, from Shakespeare to circuses and cabaret acts.

During the Fringe Festival, which starts a week before the Arts Festival, the streets of Adelaide are full of people eager to see the shows. There are so many people in Adelaide at this time, both locals and visitors, that, even with hundreds of shows, it is sometimes difficult to get a ticket.

Opposite: Wouldn't you be surprised to see these performers on the road? They are Adelaide Fringe Festival performers.

Right: This performer must have a strong pair of lungs to play at the Adelaide Arts Festival.

ANZAC DAY

The letters ANZAC stand for "Australian and New Zealand Army Corps." Anzac Day remembers the Australian and New Zealand forces who have gone to war. ANZACs were originally the soldiers who had fought a famous battle at Gallipoli in Turkey during World War I.

In memory of the ANZACs.

Since World War II, however, Anzac Day has commemorated all who contributed to any war effort that included Australia and New Zealand.

Paying respects

Anzac Day is not a celebration of war but a day for remembering those who fought or lost their lives while fighting for their country. On this day, Australians pay their respects to those who died and those who returned from wars.

A war veteran.

What happened at Gallipoli?

A solemn dawn service on Anzac Day.

During World War I, Australian and New Zealand forces fought under the command of British forces. Britain was at war with Germany, and Australia showed its loyalty to Britain by sending troops to help fight Germany and its allies.

Australian soldiers were ordered by Britain to land at Gallipoli to slow down enemy advances there. On April 25th, 1915, they landed at a place later called Anzac Cove. Conditions were extremely difficult, and many Australian soldiers were either killed or wounded. Soldiers who fought there became known for their bravery and determination.

Although they were outnumbered and suffered heavy losses, the soldiers held their ground at Gallipoli, and the Anzac legend was born.

Participating in an Anzac Day march.

Dawn services — lest we forget

Anzac Day begins with a dawn service honoring those who have died serving their country in war. As the sun rises, some people pay tributes and lay wreaths of flowers at grave sites. Others say prayers at war memorials all over the country. The service concludes with words inspired by *The Ode*, a poem written in 1914 by Laurence Binyon. A lone military bugler plays the *Last Post* as a final mark of respect.

Two-up in the trenches

A favorite pastime on Anzac Day is playing a gambling game called two-up. It is **illegal** to play two-up without a gambling license, but on Anzac Day, the authorities look the other way. The soldiers played two-up to keep spirits up at Gallipoli, so the game is a way of remembering the ANZACs.

Playing the *Last Post*.

Anzac Day marches

By mid-morning on Anzac Day, the main street of nearly every town and city in Australia is closed for the Anzac Day march. Those who have served proudly display their ribbons and medals and remember those who fought beside them and lost their lives. After the marches, many former soldiers get together at Returned and Services League clubs to have a drink and exchange stories.

Children join in

Besides watching and participating in marches, children visit people, at home or in hospitals, who are too old or too frail to attend the marches. Children also collect money on behalf of veterans and donate it to organizations that offer help to families of those killed in war. Children learn more about their country's history on Anzac Day.

Anyone who has served in the military can march in the parade, and, often, family members of those who have served also march.

Think about this

John Simpson Kirkpatrick was a medical officer who helped save many ANZAC troops at Gallipoli. With a donkey named Duffy, Kirkpatrick went out to the battlefield and helped wounded soldiers back to safety, where they could be treated. He was said to have helped up to 15 wounded soldiers a day.

MELBOURNE CUP DAY

Every year, on the first Tuesday of November, Australians celebrate a horse race called the Melbourne Cup. Held at Flemington Racecourse in Melbourne, the capital city of Victoria, this race was first run in 1861.

The race for the Melbourne Cup is often called the "race that stops a nation" because, for at least the time it takes for the race to be run, practically everyone in Australia stops to watch it, either on television or at the track. Everyone has a favorite horse. People base their choices on the horse's performances in other races, its breeding, the colors the jockey wears, or just because they like its name. Children usually are allowed to watch the race at school on television and to cheer their favorite horse home.

Look at the man's tall hat!

Having fun for the day

On Melbourne Cup Day, people enjoy picnics in the parking lot at Flemington. They arrive early to find a place at the main parking lot of the racecourse, spread out blankets, and have picnics from the trunks of their cars. Some even set up small tents and spend the day picnicking with their friends and watching races from the parking lot. People from all walks of life enjoy the party atmosphere, and everyone claims to know which horse will win the Melbourne Cup.

It is a tradition on big race days to dress up, and Melbourne Cup Day is no exception. At school, children join in the fun. Some schools even have a fancy dress day to celebrate the Melbourne Cup race.

This woman is enjoying a day at the races.

25

THINGS FOR YOU TO DO

Aborigines enjoy an extremely rich and interesting cultural tradition. Some aspects of their culture include art, singing, dancing, and storytelling.

Aboriginal art

Aboriginal art is unique and striking. Animals are featured strongly in this art, partly because they play an important role in Aboriginal life as food. Animals in Aboriginal art are usually drawn with their bones and internal organs showing. This drawing style is often called "x-ray" art. Have some fun and try your hand at drawing animals with their bones showing!

Draw some **dingoes** and have fun painting them!

Aboriginal celebrations

A *corroboree* [cuh-ROB-ah-ree] is a traditional aboriginal celebration that usually involves music and dancing. Aboriginal music is very rhythmic, and the dances either tell stories or relate aspects of Aboriginal culture. Nature and the environment are important themes of Aboriginal dances.

Keeping the Dreamtime alive

Aborigines have a rich storytelling mythology, called the Dreamtime, about the world's creation. Rules and laws of their society are kept alive through lessons learned in stories and dances. Because the Aborigines had no written language, storytelling and dance were important for them to pass their customs from one generation to the next. Evidence of large Aboriginal tribal gatherings is still found today in middens. Middens are large mounds of discarded shells at the site of a feast during a corroboree. Many Aborigines now live in or around big cities, but the tradition of dance and music is still alive. Aboriginal dance troupes combine traditional and modern techniques. They perform at festivals and theaters in Australia and around the world.

Things to look for in your library

Australia. Countries of the World (series). Peter North (Gareth Stevens, 1998).
Australia. Country Fact File (series). Robert J. Allison (Raintree/Steck-Vaughn, 1996).
Australia and Oceania. Continents (series). Kate Darian-Smith (Raintree/Steck-Vaughn, 1997).
Australia: The Southeast. (International Video Network, 1995).
Australia's Cultural Network. (http://www.acn.net.au, 1998).
Rainbow Bird: An Aboriginal Folktale from Northern Australia. Eric Maddern
  (Little, Brown and Company, 1993).
The Singing Snake. Timothy Rhodes (Hyperion Books, 1995).
Tourism Council Australia. (http://www.tourism.org.au, 1998).

MAKE CLAPPING STICKS

D uring a corroboree, Aborigines play instruments and sing to create Aboriginal music. One instrument they use is a pair of clapping sticks. Clapping sticks are easy to make, and you can decorate them with the traditional designs and patterns that make Aboriginal art unique and special.

You will need:
1. A pencil
2. A paintbrush
3. A paint tray
4. Paints
5. 2 small pieces of wood measuring 6" x 2" x 1" (15 x 5 x 2.5 cm)

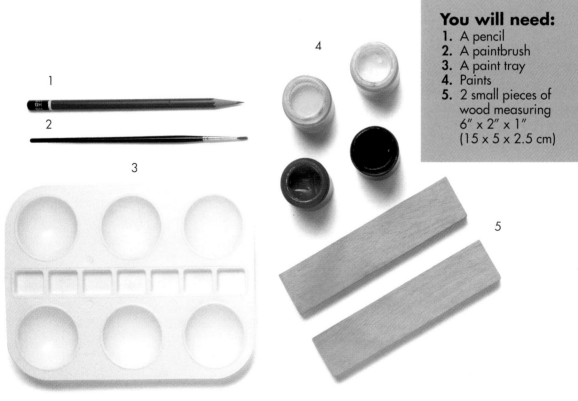

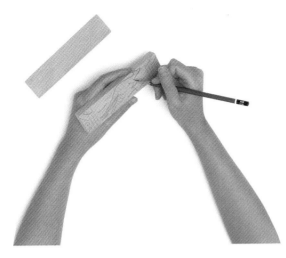

1 Use a pencil to draw designs that are patterns of dots, lines, and circles to symbolize different things, such as animals. You can follow this design of a kangaroo or come up with your own designs.

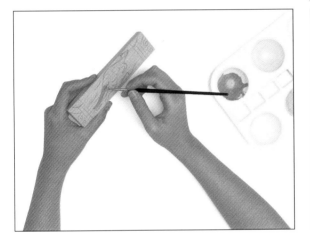

2 Paint your designs. The best colors to use are red, orange, and yellow. You can also use other colors, of course. After the paint has dried, use your clapping sticks to create different rhythms. Clap the sticks together the same way you clap your hands.

MAKE ANZAC BISCUITS

D uring World War I, ANZAC troops made biscuits from ingredients they had available to them, and Anzac biscuits became a favorite snack. Australian soldiers received packages of these biscuits from their families. The biscuits can be kept for a long time because they do not contain any milk or eggs. They are quick and simple to make. To vary the taste, add other ingredients, such as fruit or nuts.

You will need:
1. 4 tablespoons butter
2. 1 teaspoon baking soda
3. 2 tablespoons corn syrup
4. 1 cup (115 g) flour
5. 1 cup (115 g) rolled oats
6. 2 tablespoons sugar
7. Measuring spoons
8. Measuring cup
9. Metal spoon
10. Wooden spoon
11. Saucepan
12. Nonstick cookie sheet or baking pan
13. Mixing bowl

1 In a bowl, mix together the flour, rolled oats, and sugar.

2 Melt the butter in a saucepan over low heat. Stir in corn syrup and baking soda.

3 Add the butter mixture to the dry ingredients in the bowl and mix well.

4 Drop the mixture by teaspoonfuls onto the cookie sheet and flatten them. Bake the biscuits for 10 to 15 minutes at 350°F (180°C). Invite your friends to try them!

GLOSSARY

Aborigines, 4	The earliest people who lived in Australia.
alternative, 19	A choice.
amuse, 8	To entertain and keep occupied.
corroborees, 27	Traditional Aboriginal celebrations with music and dancing. Some are for either men or women only; others involve initiation ceremonies and other rites of passage in Aboriginal society.
damper, 13	Bread made with flour, water, and billy tea.
dingoes, 26	Wild dogs.
disputes, 15	Disagreements.
donate, 11	To give away either money or objects, normally for charitable purposes.
goodwill, 11	Positive regard and generosity.
illegal, 22	Against the laws of a particular country or area.
settlement, 4	Moving in and adapting to a new region or country.
witness, 3	To see an event happen.

INDEX